BASIC / NOT BORING
LANGUAGE SKILLS

SPELLING

Grades 6–8⁺

Inventive Exercises to Sharpen
Skills and Raise Achievement

Series Concept & Development
by Imogene Forte & Marjorie Frank
Exercises by Marjorie Frank

Incentive Publications, Inc.
Nashville, Tennessee

About the cover:
Bound resist, or tie dye, is the most ancient known method of fabric surface design. The brilliance of the basic tie dye design on this cover reflects the possibilities that emerge from the mastery of basic skills.

Illustrated by Kathleen Bullock
Cover art by Mary Patricia Deprez, dba Tye Dye Mary®
Cover design by Marta Drayton, Joe Shibley, and W. Paul Nance
Edited by Anna Quinn

ISBN 978-0-86530-366-9

6   7   8   9   10   11   10   09

PRINTED IN THE UNITED STATES OF AMERICA
www.incentivepublications.com

TABLE OF CONTENTS

CELEBRATE BASIC SPELLING SKILLS

Basic does not mean boring! There certainly is nothing dull about . . .

   . . . tracking down imposter letters that masquerade as other sounds

   . . . finding out where molasses, mosquitos, and zombies came from

   . . . having success spelling foods, animals, cities, jobs, and people's quirks

   . . . showing off by spelling mouthful words like *arteriosclerosis* and *phosphorescence*

   . . . deciding if you're seeing double when you read 3 double letters in *Tennessee*

   . . . getting control over that devious duo that messes up so many words: I and E

   . . . tackling troublesome words and getting the better of them

   . . . learning when to let letters be silent and when to let them speak

   . . . cleaning up outrageously misspelled headlines, titles, and letters

The idea of celebrating the basics is just what it sounds like—enjoying and improving the basic skills of spelling that increase success with reading and writing. The pages that follow are full of exercises for students that will help to review and strengthen specific skills in the content area of language arts. This is not just another "fill-in-the-blanks" way to learn. The high-interest exercises will put students to work focusing on and applying the most important skills of spelling while enjoying fun and challenging activities with words of all kinds.

The pages in this book can be used in many ways:

- for individual students to sharpen or practice a skill
- with a small group needing to relearn or strengthen a skill
- as an instructional tool for teaching a skill to any size group
- by students working on their own
- by students working under the direction of a teacher or parent

Each page may be used to introduce a new skill, to reinforce a skill, or to assess a student's performance of a skill. And, there's more than just the great student activity pages! You'll also find a hearty appendix of resources helpful for students and teachers—including a ready-to-use test for assessing these spelling skills.

As students take on the challenges of these adventures with words, they will grow in their mastery of spelling and will enjoy learning to the fullest. And as you watch them check off the basic spelling skills they've sharpened, you can celebrate with them!

SKILLS CHECKLIST FOR SPELLING

✔	SKILL	PAGE(S)
	Spell commonly misspelled words	10, 11, 16, 27, 28, 30–34, 41–46, 48–50
	Identify words that are spelled incorrectly	10, 12, 22, 31–33, 38, 39, 43, 48–50
	Correct spelling in a variety of situations	10, 12, 33, 31–33, 38, 39, 43, 45, 48–50
	Spell words that contain particularly tricky letters	12, 13, 15, 16, 26, 41–46
	Recognize and use a variety of spelling rules	12–14, 16–26
	Recognize and spell words that follow unusual rules	13
	Recognize and spell words that follow patterns	13, 15, 17, 20–25
	Spell words that break the rules	14
	Spell words that contain silent letters	16
	Spell words with prefixes	18
	Use prefixes to spell words correctly	18
	Use knowledge of roots to spell words correctly	19
	Spell words with special endings	20–23
	Use suffixes and endings to spell words correctly	20–25
	Spell words with tricky endings	24–25
	Spell and distinguish among words that look alike	27, 28, 31
	Spell and distinguish among words that sound alike	27, 28, 31
	Spell and distinguish among confusing words	27, 28, 31
	Spell words that fall into a variety of categories	27–29, 31, 33–40, 47
	Spell words of foreign origin	29
	Spell difficult words	30, 34
	Spell unusual words	30, 34
	Spell small words	33
	Spell big words	34
	Spell proper nouns that are commonly used	35

SPELLING

Skills Exercises

TROUBLE-MAKERS

These are some of the most commonly misspelled words in the English language—some of those words that are always causing trouble for spellers. Two spellers have each written the same twenty-five words below. Each word is spelled correctly on one list and misspelled on the other. Examine both lists. Cross out the MISSPELLINGS. Notice how they're misspelled. These are errors spellers frequently make in these particular words. Don't let these trouble-makers trip **you** up any more!

MEDLAND MIDDLE SCH. v. ASHFORD MIDDLE SCH.

ANNUAL SPELL-OFF

MY WORDS ARE SPELLED CORRECTLY, AND YOURS ARE NOT!

AU CONTRAIRE! I'M RIGHT AND YOU'RE WRONG!

1. business	1. buisness
2. defence	2. defense
3. receive	3. recieve
4. citizen	4. citazen
5. chocolate	5. chocalate
6. February	6. Febuary
7. lisence	7. license
8. potato	8. potatoe
9. fortunate	9. fortunite
10. enuf	10. enough
11. ocur	11. occur
12. Wensday	12. Wednesday
13. cheif	13. chief
14. exercize	14. exercise
15. summersalt	15. somersault
16. separate	16. seperate
17. cinammon	17. cinnamon
18. privilege	18. privalege
19. dinasour	19. dinosaur
20. restaurant	20. resturant
21. answer	21. anser
22. abcense	22. absence
23. benefit	23. benifit
24. advertize	24. advertise
25. suprise	25. surprise

Who has the most words spelled correctly? _____

Name

WORDS THAT PUZZLE

Here are fifteen of those words that constantly puzzle spellers. One set of numbered puzzle pieces gives you the beginnings of these tricky words. Another set of pieces gives you a clue for a word. After reading each clue, finish spelling the word correctly. On the matching puzzle piece, finish spelling the word correctly.

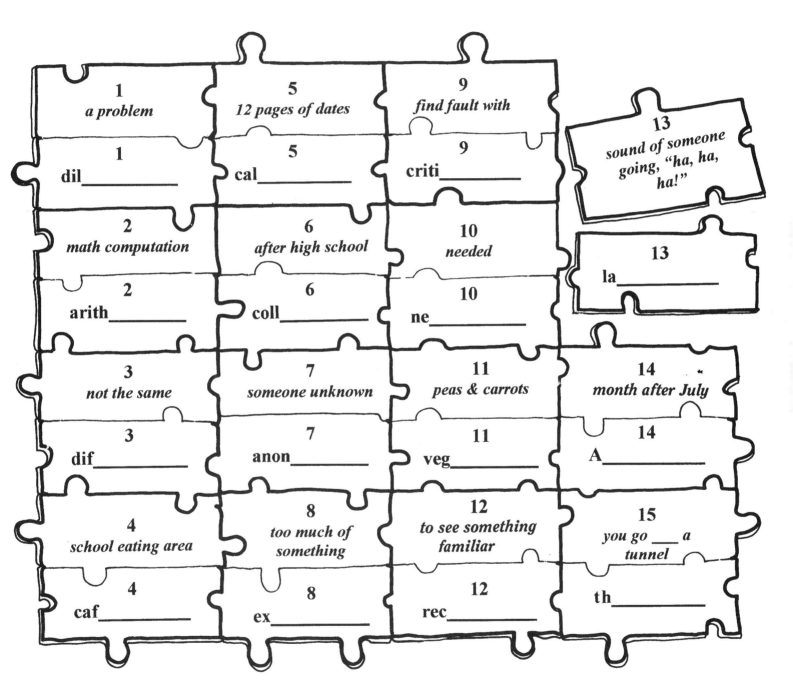

1 — a problem
1 — dil_____

5 — 12 pages of dates
5 — cal_____

9 — find fault with
9 — criti_____

13 — sound of someone going, "ha, ha, ha!"
13 — la_____

2 — math computation
2 — arith_____

6 — after high school
6 — coll_____

10 — needed
10 — ne_____

3 — not the same
3 — dif_____

7 — someone unknown
7 — anon_____

11 — peas & carrots
11 — veg_____

14 — month after July
14 — A_____

4 — school eating area
4 — caf_____

8 — too much of something
8 — ex_____

12 — to see something familiar
12 — rec_____

15 — you go ____ a tunnel
15 — th_____

Name _____

SEEING DOUBLE

Daniel thinks he's seeing double when he sees all the double letters in the words below. Do they belong? Are the right letters doubled? Is he seeing double, or are these letters supposed to be doubled? Decide if each word should have a double letter and if the letter doubled is correct. If a word is **not** correct, rewrite it correctly. (Some mistakes do not involve double letters.)

MAYBE I NEED NEW GLASSES!

nn tt pp pp mm oo

1. butterscotch_____
2. caterpillar_____
3. bennefit _____
4. zipper _____
5. accountant_____
6. annimal _____
7. dessert _____
8. ommitted _____
9. embarass _____
10. misspell _____
11. quizzacal _____
12. chauffeur _____
13. bizarre _____
14. basaar _____
15. cerreal _____
16. mousse_____
17. ammonnia _____
18. travelling _____
19. comma _____
20. paralell _____
21. mammal_____

22. horrid_____
23. ballott_____
24. barracudda_____
25. ballcony _____
26. boycott_____
27. annual _____
28. rudder _____
29. carrot _____
30. memmory _____
31. cellophane _____
32. oppossum_____
33. hipoppottamus_____
34. staccatto_____
35. Tenessee_____
36. penniless _____
37. cenntennial _____
38. anniversary _____
39. proffessor _____
40. cellebrate _____

Name _____

12

A DEVIOUS DUO

Here are two letters that are hazardous to spellers when they get together. You've heard the rule:

LET ME SEE NOW, HOW DOES THAT RULE GO?

I before E
Except after C
Or when sounding like A
As in "neighbor" or "weigh"

Usually follow this rule—but not always. Practice using the rule on the words below. Write a word with **I** and **E** in it to match each clue. Then do the activity on page 14, where you'll practice breaking some rules.

1. fr_____ t
2. sl _____ h
3. n _____ hood
4. mis _____ f
5. ach _____ e
6. r _____ n
7. con _____ ce
8. con _____ ted
9. quo _____ t
10. p _____ e
11. soc _____ y
12. eff _____ nt
13. gr _____ f
14. sc _____ ce
15. _____ ght
16. w _____ t
17. defi _____ nt
18. con _____ nt
19. hy _____ ne
20. shr _____ k

1. kind of a train
2. Santa owns one
3. place to live
4. naughtiness
5. to accomplish
6. king does this
7. tells you right from wrong
8. stuck-up
9. answer to division
10. eat a _____ of cake or pizza
11. huge group of people
12. opposite of sloppy and wasteful
13. sadness
14. subject with a lab
15. after seven
16. number on a scale
17. lacking
18. easy and accessible
19. personal cleanliness
20. piercing scream

Name _____

RULE BREAKERS

Sometimes words break the rules, and you just have to remember which ones are the rule breakers. Get to know these rule breakers below. First read the three rules. Decide if each word below breaks one of these rules. On the line after the word, write the number of the rule it breaks. Then practice the word by writing it again.

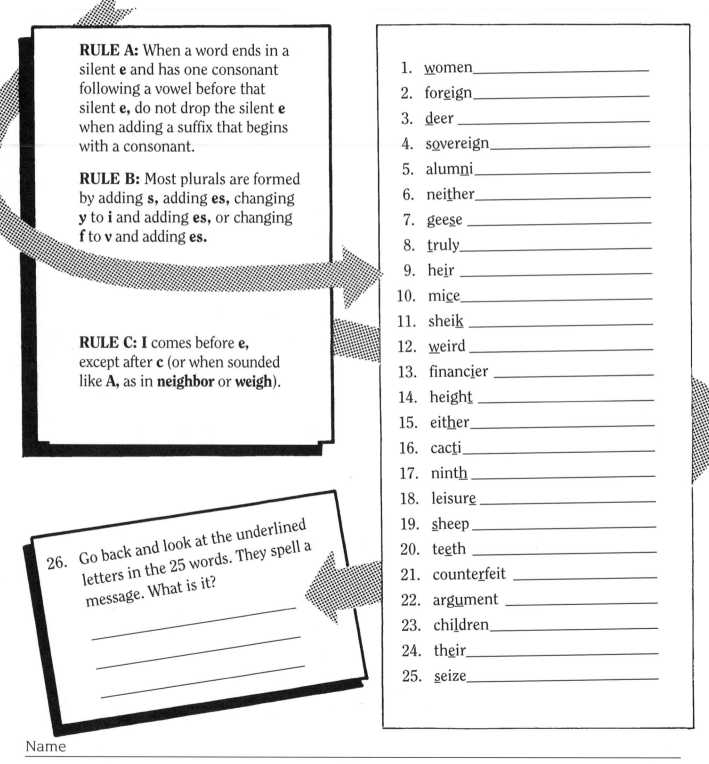

RULE A: When a word ends in a silent **e** and has one consonant following a vowel before that silent **e,** do not drop the silent **e** when adding a suffix that begins with a consonant.

RULE B: Most plurals are formed by adding **s,** adding **es,** changing **y** to **i** and adding **es,** or changing **f** to **v** and adding **es.**

RULE C: I comes before **e,** except after **c** (or when sounded like **A,** as in **neighbor** or **weigh**).

1. women_____
2. foreign_____
3. deer _____
4. sovereign_____
5. alumni_____
6. neither_____
7. geese _____
8. truly_____
9. heir _____
10. mice_____
11. sheik _____
12. weird _____
13. financier _____
14. height _____
15. either_____
16. cacti_____
17. ninth _____
18. leisure _____
19. sheep_____
20. teeth _____
21. counterfeit _____
22. argument _____
23. children_____
24. their_____
25. seize_____

26. Go back and look at the underlined letters in the 25 words. They spell a message. What is it?

_____
_____
_____

Name _____

14

THE OUTRAGEOUS O

Lots of words have **O**s inside them. **O**s make words fun, interesting to look at, and wonderful to say. They also make words tricky to spell. These clues hint at words with at least two **O**s in them. But where do the **O**s go? Use the clue to decide what the word is. Then write the word with the right number of **O**s in the right places!

1. (a slogan)	2. (opposite of remembered)	3. (moth hatches from one)	4. (smell)	5. (opposite of rare)	6. (tropical storm)
M _____	F _____	C _____	O _____	C _____	M _____
7. (picture)	8. (study of poisonous stuff)	9. (guaranteed; won't fail)	10. (trail behind)	11. (insignia)	12. (skin design)
PH _____	T _____	F _____	F _____	L _____	T _____

Olive Ordered Oranges One October.

13. (to view from above)	14. (ducklike bird)	15. (train engine)	16. (whistlelike instrument)	17. (speaker)	18. (one-lens eyeglass)
O _____	L _____	L _____	K _____	O _____	M _____
19. (holey, like a sponge)	20. (African magic)	21. (stinging arachnid)	22. (foe)	23. (no longer a freshman)	24. (boring)
P _____	V _____	S _____	O _____	S _____	M _____

Name _____

THE SILENT TREATMENT

Some letters hang around in words and make themselves seen, but they can't be heard. They don't add any sound to the word at all. Each of these titles for stories, articles, or essays has one or more words with silent letters. Look at them carefully. Then complete each title by writing in a word with the silent treatment.

1. Life in the _____ of the Inner City

2. Rising _____ Takes over Bakery

3. Rat _____ Power Lines

4. Why You Should Give _____ to Pigeons

5. Children Laugh at _____ (Rhymes with Zoo)

6. Police Find Money _____ in Newspaper

7. Circuit Court _____ Rules Golden Gate _____ Safe

8. Congress Asks; President _____ , "NO!"

9. Governor _____ , Effective Immediately

10. King Arthur's Favorite _____ Steals Famous Silver _____

11. Bear Eats Red _____ from Mayor's Bush

12. Diners Suffer from _____ Poisoning

13. Butcher Bakes Carving _____ into Wedding Cake

14. Tests Show Third Graders Are Smart, Not _____

15. Children _____ Allegiance to the Flag

16. The Hunter Who _____ the Grizzly for Six Weeks

17. Policeman Drops Shiny _____ Down City Drainpipe

18. The Sheep Who Birthed Thirty-Three _____

19. Always _____ before You Enter

20. King _____ for Eighty Years

MAYBE I SHOULD HAVE TAKEN THE LITTLE ONE.

Name _____

"F" IN DISGUISE

The sound that F makes is not always made by F. Sometimes it's made by impostors—phony Fs! Usually the impostor is Double Agent PHRANKIE PHRENCH or Double Agent RALGH RATLOUGH. Both of these agents pose as other sounds in other words.

Each of these words can be finished correctly by one of these impostors. Tell which one by filling in **ph** or **gh** to complete each word.

1. ____ONY

2. SI____ON

3. GRA____ING

4. ENOU____

5. SYM____ONY

6. ROU____

7. ____ONICS

8. LAU____TER

9. EM____ASIS

10. TOU____

11. ____OBIA

12. ____YSICAL

13. COU____

14. STEREO____ONIC

15. TRIUM____ANT

16. XYLO____ONE

17. TROU____

18. ____ILOSO____Y

Name

TO BEGIN WITH...

Thousands of words begin with a handful of little beginning word parts called prefixes. If you know how to recognize these and spell them, you'll have a good beginning on the road to spelling success. When you know about prefixes, you can take a word apart and the spelling will be much easier.

In this assignment, you know the beginnings. You just have to track down the rest of the words and spell them right! Follow the clues. Match each clue to a prefix and finish the word.

biblio_____

in_____

dis_____

tri_____

ad_____

extra_____

ultra_____

anti_____

CLUES

1. doctor's orders
2. leave out
3. do the essay again
4. alikeness in form
5. leave
6. break down into parts
7. change to another language
8. tiny piece inside a computer
9. make last longer
10. not able to be seen
11. go ahead of
12. written list of books
13. beyond ordinary
14. exceptional sound
15. not approve
16. cycle with three wheels
17. against war
18. not tied

un_____

ex_____

re_____

con_____

de_____

sub_____

trans_____

micro_____

pro_____

pre_____

Name

AT THE ROOT OF IT

You may not think of words as living things with roots. But roots are places from which words grow—sort of like plants. Words have roots as the "center" of their structure, and often other parts, such as prefixes, endings, and suffixes, are added on. Another important thing about a root is that it supplies the basic meaning of the word.

These words are missing their roots. The meaning of each **root** is given; see if you can fill in the missing root to hold the word together. Spell the roots correctly!

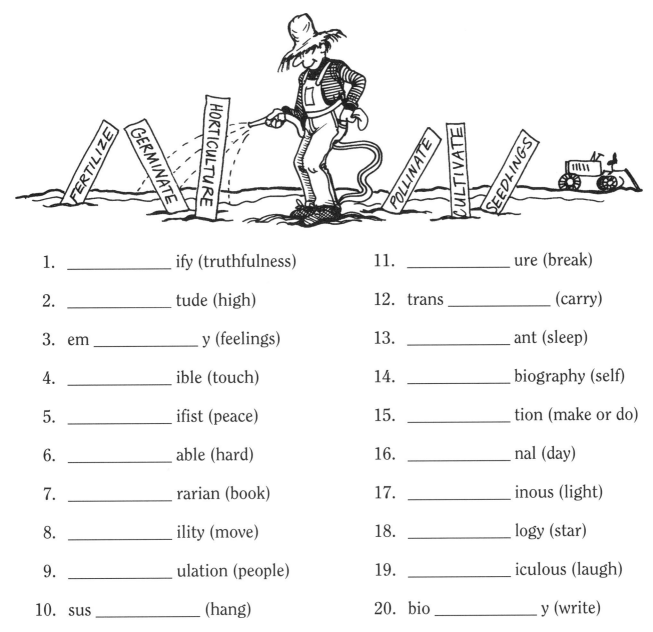

1. _____ ify (truthfulness)

2. _____ tude (high)

3. em _____ y (feelings)

4. _____ ible (touch)

5. _____ ifist (peace)

6. _____ able (hard)

7. _____ rarian (book)

8. _____ ility (move)

9. _____ ulation (people)

10. sus _____ (hang)

11. _____ ure (break)

12. trans _____ (carry)

13. _____ ant (sleep)

14. _____ biography (self)

15. _____ tion (make or do)

16. _____ nal (day)

17. _____ inous (light)

18. _____ logy (star)

19. _____ iculous (laugh)

20. bio _____ y (write)

Name _____

SPELLING "ANT"-ICS

Ants are everywhere! So are words with **ants** in them. Every clue below tells about an **ant** word (a word that ends with an "ant"). See if you can get all twenty. Write the whole word, and spell it correctly—make sure the **ant** is at the end.

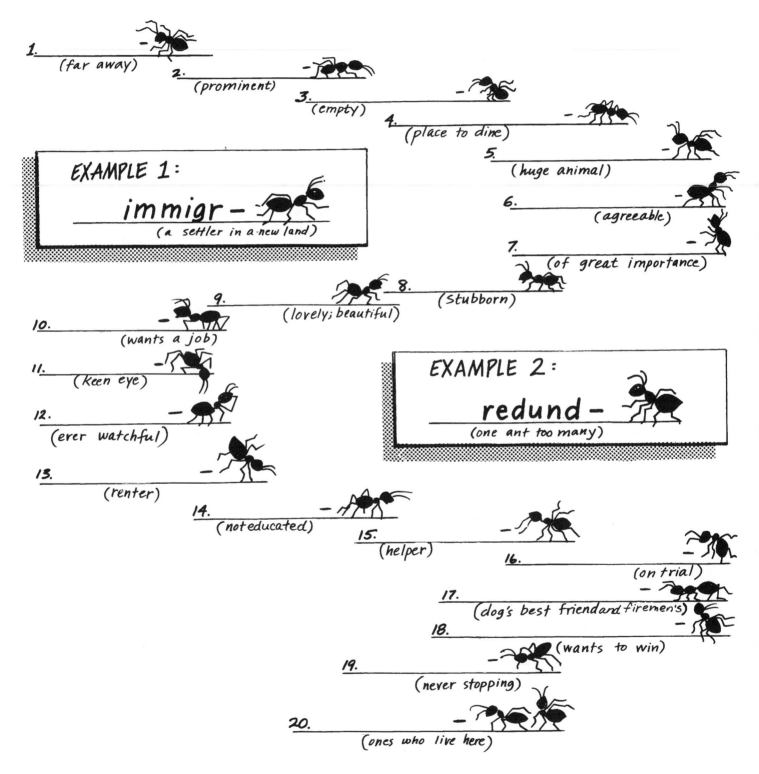

1. _____ (far away)

2. _____ (prominent)

3. _____ (empty)

4. _____ (place to dine)

5. _____ (huge animal)

6. _____ (agreeable)

7. _____ (of great importance)

EXAMPLE 1:
immigr- _____ (a settler in a new land)

8. _____ (stubborn)

9. _____ (lovely; beautiful)

10. _____ (wants a job)

11. _____ (keen eye)

12. _____ (erer watchful)

13. _____ (renter)

EXAMPLE 2:
redund- _____ (one ant too many)

14. _____ (not educated)

15. _____ (helper)

16. _____ (on trial)

17. _____ (dog's best friend and firemen's)

18. _____ (wants to win)

19. _____ (never stopping)

20. _____ (ones who live here)

Name _____

20

EDIBLE ENDINGS

EAT and ATE keep turning up in lots of words. Maybe it's because, as language developed, people were always thinking about their favorite pastime—eating. These two endings finish off many good words—like dessert finishes off a good meal. The trouble is, people often get them mixed up. Every one of these words can be completed with **eat** or **ate**. Finish each one with the correct ending.

EAT   ATE

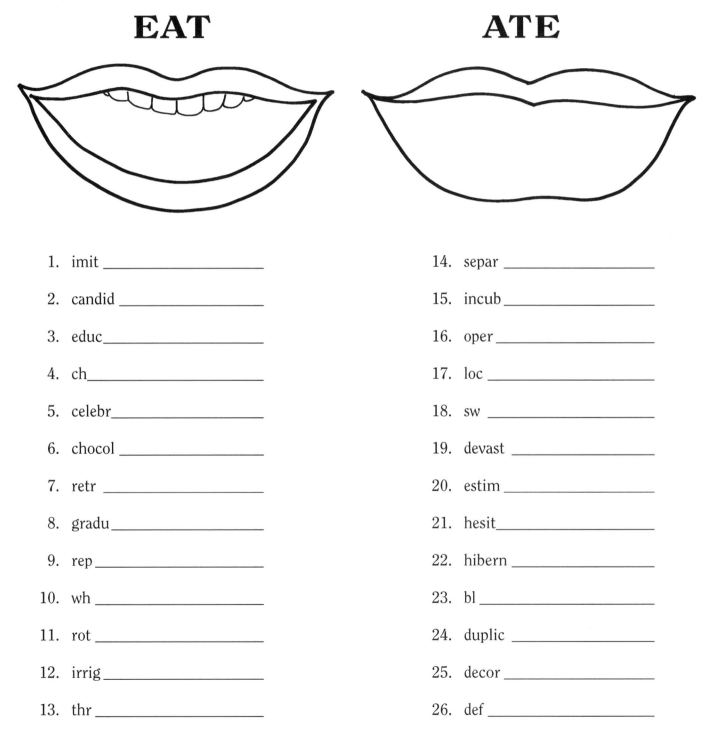

1. imit _____

2. candid _____

3. educ_____

4. ch_____

5. celebr_____

6. chocol _____

7. retr _____

8. gradu_____

9. rep _____

10. wh _____

11. rot _____

12. irrig_____

13. thr _____

14. separ _____

15. incub_____

16. oper _____

17. loc _____

18. sw _____

19. devast _____

20. estim _____

21. hesit_____

22. hibern _____

23. bl _____

24. duplic _____

25. decor _____

26. def _____

Name _____

Basic Skills/Spelling 6-8+

A MESS IN THE END

AL, **EL**, and **LE** just get mixed up all the time by spellers. And it's happened again. Some of these words are spelled correctly. Others have an **EL** where an **AL** or **LE** should be, or an **AL** where an **EL** or an **LE** should be, or an **LE** where an **AL** or an **EL** should be! Whew! What a mess! Please straighten it out. If the word is correct, give it a star. If it has the wrong ending, cross it out and write the correct one.

1. wrestel
2. hystericel
3. candell
4. principel
5. practical
6. oral
7. brutal
8. level
9. angel
10. icicle
11. cancel
12. rural
13. unravel
14. legel
15. wrestel
16. spirel
17. clavical
18. level
19. VESSLE
20. parole
21. channal
22. fatal
23. visibal
24. RADICEL
25. cynical
26. MODEL
27. medle
28. OBSTACAL
29. level
30. travel
31. tentacle
32. CARNIVEL

WATCH YOUR TAIL!

A huge number of spelling errors happen because the spellers aren't watching their tails (the tails of their words, that is). Endings really can trip you up. Here are nine different three-letter endings. Which one is the right one for each word?

Look at each word beginning below. Decide which "tail" is the right one for it, and write it (with its correct ending) in the place where it belongs. (See "tails" in the drawing below.)

1. apolog _____
2. host _____
3. infant _____
4. fugit _____
5. varn _____
6. telev _____
7. optim _____
8. self _____
9. child _____
10. negat _____
11. punit _____
12. pessim _____
13. juven _____
14. fool _____
15. pol _____

16. abol _____
17. expens _____
18. critic _____
19. exerc _____
20. defens _____
21. cynic _____
22. styl _____
23. optim _____
24. burglar _____
25. opportun _____
26. initial _____
27. favor _____
28. dent _____
29. flor _____

Name _____

Basic Skills/Spelling 6-8+

23

Copyright ©1997 by Incentive Publications, Inc., Nashville, TN.

TRICKY ENDINGS

How do you spell **confusion?** . . . Is it **confution? confucion? confucian?** And how do you spell **genius?** . . . **genus? genious? geneous?** It doesn't take a spelling genius to clear up the confusion. It just takes some practice with the tricky endings that confuse spellers. Practice spelling words that end with these:

ion tion sion cian tune us ious eous ius uous

Look at the words in the columns below. Finish each word with the correct ending chosen from the corresponding cards. Then write the number of the word on the correct card with its matching ending.

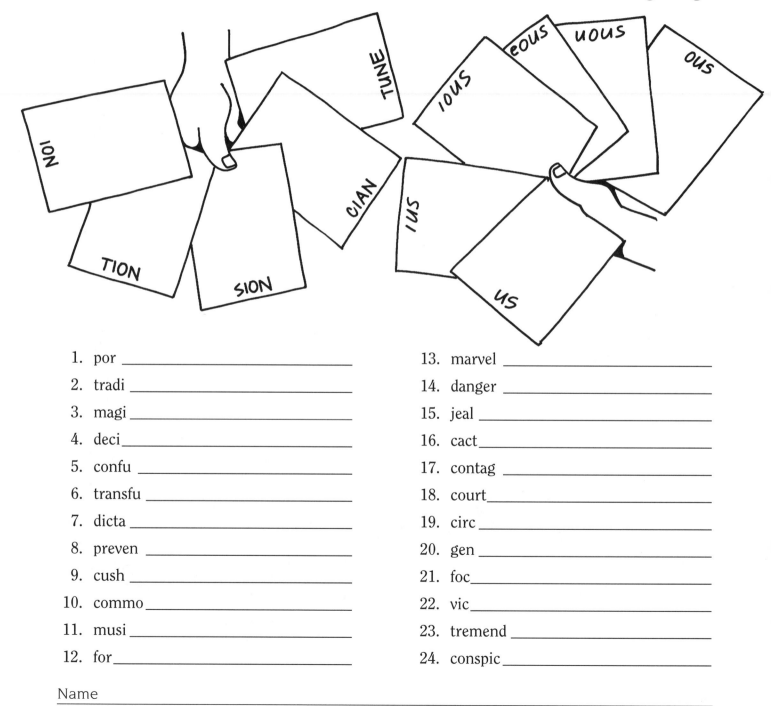

1. por _____

2. tradi _____

3. magi _____

4. deci _____

5. confu _____

6. transfu _____

7. dicta _____

8. preven _____

9. cush _____

10. commo _____

11. musi _____

12. for _____

13. marvel _____

14. danger _____

15. jeal _____

16. cact _____

17. contag _____

18. court _____

19. circ _____

20. gen _____

21. foc _____

22. vic _____

23. tremend _____

24. conspic _____

Name _____

MORE TRICKY ENDINGS

Do you know **ible** from **able** and **ence** from **ance**? To be an accurate speller, you'd better know which words require which endings. Here are some more words to practice. Finish the words in the columns below with the correct ending chosen from the cards. Then write the number of each word on the card where it belongs.

1. neglig _____
2. consequ _____
3. nuis _____
4. sci _____
5. sequ _____
6. adolesc _____
7. eleg _____
8. appli _____
9. abs _____
10. reli _____
11. evid _____
12. turbul _____
13. attend _____
14. insur _____
15. occurr _____

16. imposs _____
17. revers _____
18. communic _____
19. notice _____
20. tang _____
21. permiss _____
22. depend _____
23. reli _____
24. sens _____
25. tang _____
26. desir _____
27. leg _____
28. ador _____
29. dispos _____
30. invis _____

♠ ENCE ♦

♥ ANCE ♣

♠ ABLE ♦

♥ IBLE ♣

Name

25

TROUBLE IN THE MIDDLE

Do you ever get lost in the middle of a word? You know how it starts, you know how it ends, but somewhere in the middle things fall apart? It seems that the beginnings and endings of words get all the attention! But what's in the middle is pretty crucial to correct spelling.

Get better at middles by practicing these words that have tricky vowel combinations inside them. The middles are firmly in place this time. Figure out the rest of the word that surrounds these CORRECT middles.

GROAN... WHY DID I EAT THOSE VOWELS?

1. great pain   __ __ __ ui __ __

2. great confusion   __ __ ao __

3. dangerous   __ __ ea __ __ __ __ __ __

4. a fake   __ __ au __

5. very poor person   __ au __ __ __

6. no rain for a long time   __ __ ou __ __ __

7. a large cat   __ ou __ __

8. place to find synonyms   __ __ __ __ au __

9. a prejudice   __ ia __

10. loud, noisy   __ oi __ __ __ __ __ __

11. color that hides an animal   __ __ __ ou __ __ __ __ __

12. believable   __ __ au __ __ __ __ __

13. impressive speaker   __ __ __ __ ue __ __

14. fish home   __ __ ua __ __ __ __

15. spicy hotdog   __ au __ __ __ __

16. facial hair   __ ea __ __

17. big cat with spots   __ eo __ __ __

18. white, cabbage-tasting vegetable   __ au __ __ __ __ __ __ __ __

19. epidemic sickness   __ __ __ __ ue __ __ __

20. opposed to   __ __ ai __ __ __

21. idea   __ __ ou __ __ __

22. fake identity   __ __ __ __ ui __ __

Name

LOOK-ALIKES & SOUND ALIKES

Which is underage . . . a **minor** or a **miner**? On a dark night in a dark alley . . . are you likely to be **scared** or **sacred**? Who runs the school . . . the **principal** or the **principle**? Is Washington D.C. the Unites States' **capital** or **capitol**? And do you and your friends look for adventure **altogether** or **all together**? Words that look or sound exactly alike or similar are the cause of many spelling errors. Here's a chance to get some of them straightened out. Choose the correct word from the box to fit in each space.

1. Jaycee is 15. She doesn't work in a mine. She is a _____ .

2. On a dark night in a dark alley, you'll probably be feeling _____ and thinking that your life is very _____ to you.

3. The bold, ambitious knight from King Arthur's court had one favorite steel _____ , which he left to his favorite _____ after he died.

4. The school _____ reported 22 _____ of food-throwing in the cafeteria last month. She noted that the _____ of these episodes had doubled since September. As a result, she declared that _____ would no longer be served at the end of school lunches.

5. If a bike doesn't have a _____ , it will be extremely hard to _____ up the hill to the high school.

6. If a _____ in your classroom dove off a 50-foot _____ into the ocean, would you be likely to do the same?

7. On my vacation, I _____ in a glider, rode a camel across a _____ , and helped a _____ pan for gold.

8. Magda decided that, for her visit to the _____ city of her state and the _____ building, she would dye her _____ blue, the color of her state bird.

9. _____ , I have collected seven different varieties of scorpions (all dead, of course!).

10. When my sister becomes president, as I know she will, I'll write her a letter of congratulations on the _____ she designed for me when she was in kindergarten.

soared	stationary	principal	stationery
pier	all together	scared	incidence
sacred	desert	pedal	capitol
peer	sword	hair	miner
capital	incidents	peddle	altogether
minor	dessert	principle	heir

Name _____

Basic Skills/Spelling 6-8+

MORE LIKELY ALIKE

Should you seize the daze . . . or seas the days? Is a lyre untruthful . . . or a carrot valuable? Do colonels get kernels stuck in their teeth . . . or is it kernels that give military orders? Here are some more of those words that look alike, sound alike, or are so similar that they trip you up on spelling. Write a question or sentence that uses each group of words.

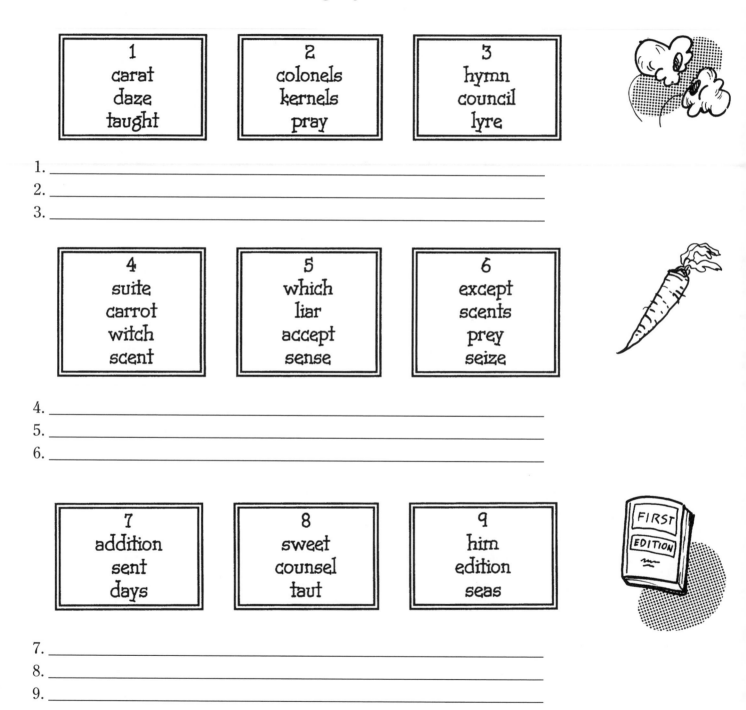

1
carat
daze
taught

2
colonels
kernels
pray

3
hymn
council
lyre

1. _____
2. _____
3. _____

4
suite
carrot
witch
scent

5
which
liar
accept
sense

6
except
scents
prey
seize

4. _____
5. _____
6. _____

7
addition
sent
days

8
sweet
counsel
taut

9
him
edition
seas

7. _____
8. _____
9. _____

Name _____

28

BORROWED WORDS

Thousands of English words that we use daily are borrowed from other languages. They add a rich flavor to our language. Here are just a few of the words that found their way to us across seas and borders.

algebra (Arabic)
antique (French)
blitz (German)
bourgeois (French)
buoy (Dutch)
chauffeur (French)
chemistry (Arabic)
elite (French)
emerald (French)
freight (Dutch)
guru (Indian)

gorilla (African)
kindergarten (German)
lasso (Spanish)
macaroni (Italian)
magazine (Arabic)
molasses (Portuguese)
mosquito (Spanish)
mandarin (Chinese)
mustang (Spanish)
pajama (Indian)
paradise (Persian)

piano (Italian)
sarong (India)
sauerkraut (German)
shampoo (Indian)
tambourine (Arabic)
tourniquet (French)
tsar (Russian)
tycoon (Japanese)
vanilla (Spanish)
veto (Latin)
yacht (Dutch)
zombie (African)

Find a word (or words) above that matches each meaning. Write the word on the line, and make sure you spell it correctly.

1. precious gemstone_____
2. biting insect_____
3. Italian food_____
4. school for young children _____
5. things that float _____
6. school subjects_____
7. old and valuable _____
8. something to read _____
9. German food _____
10. an ultimate environment _____
11. animals_____
12. clothing _____
13. say "no" to _____
14. music makers _____

Name

WILD, WEIRD, & WACKY WORDS

Some words are just plain weird—or outrageous—or unusual. It might be because of the way they look, or sound, or are spelled. It might be because of their meanings. And, of course, different people have different opinions about what makes a word weird.

Here are some unusual words. Say each one to yourself, because they sound interesting. Write each one, spelling it correctly. Then find out what 10 of them mean (all, if you want).

BIZARRE etiquette & supercilious OGRES WITH lorgnettes:

PETIT-FOURS ?

HUMPH

WE ONLY EAT STURGEON PATÉ,

OR, LADY-FINGERS

etiquette _____

bizarre _____

ogre _____

kazoo _____

morgue _____

lozenge _____

catastrophe _____

niche _____

incisors _____

rogue _____

cipher _____

tongue _____

hyperbole _____

elixir _____

blasé _____

facsimile _____

etcetera _____

dungeon _____

pathos _____

menagerie _____

bamboozle _____

anachronism _____

sousaphone _____

petit fours _____

sturgeon _____

paté _____

jodhpurs _____

supercilious _____

onomatopoeia _____

lorgnette _____

Name _____

WORDS THAT CONFUSE

I always loose my notes when I get ready for a test, accept for math, because I warp my lunch in those and always have them near. My mother gives me unending advise about how to get thorough this problem, but, I insure you, it's a useless excise. It'll be major croupe if I ever get excepted into any collage.

I. This writer is confused—help him! Rewrite his paragraph (above) and replace the wrong words with the correctly spelled words he meant to use.

_____

_____

_____

_____

II. Next, help him with his spelling assignment. Locate each word that is incorrect. Cross it out and replace it with the correctly spelled word he should have chosen.

1. If I could just get trough this week, I can get though anything! _____

2. I wonder weather the whether will get any better. _____ _____

3. The district attorney decided to persecute the clown for failing to make people laugh.
   _____

4. My mother never knows witch buttons to push on the remote control for the VCR.
   _____

5. I certainly could use a guardian angle today (particularly one who knows geometry).
   _____

6. My English teacher says I have a serious lack of comas in my essay. _____

7. My older brother is always threatening to afflict pain on me if I don't get off the
   telephone. _____

8. Jeanie inferred to Michelle that she was going to the prom with Joe. _____

9. You got one hundred on your science test? That's inedible! _____

10. As you can see by how outgoing I am, I'm definitely an introvert. _____

Name _____

HOW TO TURN A FLEA INTO A LEAF

It isn't really all that hard to turn a **flea** into a **leaf**! Just rearrange the letters in the **flea**, and you get a **leaf**. Once you know how to spell many words correctly, you can have fun with them by moving the letters around to get new words. Each of these sentences below is a bit of a puzzle for you. Fill in each blank by making a new (correctly spelled) word from the letters in the CAPITALIZED word.

1. The grave-robbers were SCARED when they entered the
_____ tomb of the ancient Egyptian Pharaoh.

2. In many old myths and fairy tales, people go in search of
CURES to reverse a _____ .

3. It breaks my HEART to see how pollution has ruined some
parts of the _____ .

4. "LISTEN for a moment," urged the wilderness guide. But to our unattuned ears, the
snowy woods were _____ .

5. "Don't ride over any kind of rough _____ ," cautioned the horse TRAINER.

6. I just _____ going into that haunted house. No one else has DARED to do it!

7. "Every winter, on the first moonless NIGHT," whispered the storyteller, the
_____ in the lagoon begins an eerie howling that lasts till dawn.

8. A SONIC boom rattled the house of the Greek man, and his _____ fell off
the wall.

9. If you run into a leprechaun on MARCH 17th, he might just _____ the gold
out of your teeth.

10. My father RAGES when the _____ freeze on his snowmobile.

11. Scientists are ALERT to the fact that radiation can _____ chromosomes
in certain laboratory rats.

12. Greg complained about his MENTAL abilities in a long _____ to his
math teacher.

13. If you pay attention to what I'm trying to _____ you, you won't need to
CHEAT on tests.

Name _____

SMALL PROBLEMS

Problems can come in small packages. Many of the most commonly misspelled words are little ones. Some small words trouble people all their lives! Get a handle on these small words now, so they won't turn into big spelling problems for you later on. Here are fifty-one small words that you use all the time. This guy has spelled all but two of them incorrectly. Identify the two correct words, and spell the others correctly for him.

1. abowt
2. abov
3. acke
4. aftter
5. alilke
6. allmost
7. allready
8. allways
9. arne't
10. atach
11. ahful
12. balence
13. bottel
14. brige
15. bary
16. sertin
17. cheif

18. choise
19. coler
20. dary
21. doller
22. dout
23. ege
24. enuf
25. field
26. fourty
27. gost
28. gues
29. hopeing
30. iland
31. juise
32. nock
33. lauf
34. lenth

35. lovly
36. obay
37. ofen
38. peple
39. peice
40. probaly
41. recieve
42. raize
43. safty
44. sence
45. stomack
46. Tusday
47. twoard
48. usful
49. vary
50. wen
51. whoze

Name

THESE ARE A MOUTHFUL

Don't be intimidated by big words—even if they fill up your mouth when you try to say them. Sometimes big words are even easier to spell than small words. Just break them down into small parts and spell them one piece at a time.

Practice spelling these mouthful words by asking someone else to say them to you, slowly, in syllables. Write them until you have them under your control! (By the way, if you don't know what some of these mean—find out! Never write a word that you don't understand.)

Name

NAMES TO KNOW

There are thousands of them! People! Places! Events! Organizations! Things! Whenever a proper name is used, it's called a **proper noun.** These are all capitalized. This directory lists several proper nouns. They are all words you should know how to spell. The problem is, the words are missing. Fill them in (using the clues to the right), and spell them correctly. You will probably need a dictionary to help you out.

#		Clue
1.	A _____	city in New Mexico
2.	A _____	coldest continent
3.	A _____	month after July
4.	B _____	capital of Idaho
5.	B _____	writing for the blind
6.	C _____	world-selling soda pop
7.	C _____	explored America, 1492
8.	C _____	south of Massachusetts
9.	D _____	document that set off the Revolutionary War
10.	D _____	U.S. political party
11.	D _____	capital of Iowa
12.	D _____	U.S. capital
13.	E _____	country east of Algeria
14.	E _____	U.S. president before Nixon
15.	F _____	month after January
16.	H _____	city—site of atomic bomb
17.	H _____	country east of Austria
18.	L _____	U.S. president in Civil War
19.	L _____	largest city in California
20.	M _____	north of Connecticut
21.	M _____	state north of Wisconsin
22.	M _____	sea south of France
23.	N _____	city—site of atomic bomb
24.	P _____	world's largest ocean
25.	P _____	cuts across isthmus in Central America
26.	P _____	government body in England
27.	P _____	newcomers to America
28.	R _____	river between U.S. & Mexico
29.	R _____	U.S. political party
30.	R _____	country west of Ukraine
31.	S _____	site of Golden Gate Bridge
32.	S _____	stands above NY harbor
33.	T _____	capital of Florida
34.	T _____	33° S of equator
35.	T _____	day after Monday
36.	T _____	king of dinosaurs
37.	V _____	capital of British Columbia
38.	V _____	country south of Paraguay
39.	W _____	day after Tuesday
40.	Z _____	country in center of Africa

Name

AARDVARKS & EMUS

Use the clues to lead you to the correct animal names. Write them down and spell them correctly, and you will be able to answer the question below. Write the letter that matches each number in the correct space at the bottom to solve the puzzle.

1. a long, narrow tropical fish with protruding jaws __ __ __ __ __ __ __ __ __ __
    $\qquad\qquad\qquad\qquad\qquad\qquad$ 1 $\qquad\qquad\qquad$ 8

2. a big cat with spots __ __ __ __ __ __ __ __
    $\qquad\qquad\qquad$ 10

3. a big, black, fast-running cat __ __ __ __ __ __ __ __
    $\qquad\qquad\qquad$ 3

4. ivory tusks and big feet __ __ __ __ __ __ __ __
    $\qquad\qquad\qquad\qquad\qquad\qquad$ 7

5. long neck, but makes no sound __ __ __ __ __ __ __
    $\qquad\qquad\qquad\qquad\qquad$ 2 11

6. danger in the swamp __ __ __ __ __ __ __ __ __
    $\qquad\qquad\qquad$ 16

7. howls at the moon __ __ __ __ __ __
    $\qquad\qquad$ 6

8. feeds on dead animals __ __ __ __ __ __ __

9. eats wood in your house __ __ __ __ __ __ __
    $\qquad\qquad\qquad$ 9

10. huge, tough-skinned animal with one horn __ __ __ __ __ __ __ __ __ __
    $\qquad\qquad\qquad\qquad\qquad$ 16

11. now extinct __ __ __ __ __ __ __ __
    $\qquad\qquad$ 14

12. changes colors __ __ __ __ __ __ __ __ __
    $\qquad$ 5

13. large, wide-mouthed African mammal __ __ __ __ __ __ __ __ __ __ __ __
    $\qquad\qquad\qquad\qquad\qquad$ 17

14. an ape with shaggy, reddish-brown coat and no tail __ __ __ __ __ __ __ __ __ __ __
    $\qquad\qquad\qquad\qquad\qquad\qquad\qquad\qquad$ 4

15. plays dead; hangs upside-down __ __ __ __ __ __ __
    $\qquad\qquad$ 12

16. large, hairy, tropical spider __ __ __ __ __ __ __ __

17. stinging arachnid __ __ __ __ __ __ __ __
    $\qquad\qquad$ 13

18. carries packs in steep terrain __ __ __ __ __

19. animal with stripes __ __ __ __ __
    15

I'M LOOKING FOR THE MENAGERIE. (WHATEVER THAT IS)

What is a menagerie?

__ __ __ __ __ __ __ __ __ __
1   2   3   4   5   6   7   8   9   10

__ __ __ __ __ __ __
11   12   13   14   15   16   17

Name

WORDS ON THE JOB

This puzzle is full of words that go to work every day—names of workers in different jobs and professions. See if you can find at least twenty. (There are 34.) Write these, spelled correctly, in the space below the puzzle.

```
D F I N A N C I E R B A N K E R X C F
A T T O R N E Y S S E R T C A N V O I
N T U R P M I S C D R A U G E F I L R
C V U T P T K L R E T N E P R A C W E
E L B H E G H M O R E B M U L P I A F
R E C O R G H A R O G D A R E H N I I
C L O D R D I H M A N A G E R A A T G
O L M O N B E P R O F E S S O R H E H
O M I N I S T E R I L U Y S S M C R T
K X C T O K J D B N O O S S A A E C E
F Y T I S A V B U S I N G E R C M M R
P H Y S I C I S T C M O P I P I S D S
R O K T C T C M C H U I N P S S O B U
O P H T H O K A H L S C U L P T O R R
T O O K C R O Y E M I S S T E R I H G
A N K C H O P O R I C K L K J U D G E
N O E L E C T R I C I A N S A S H E O
E O P Y F H E C B E A U T I C I A N N
S L O R E H C A E T N U R S E P H G O
```

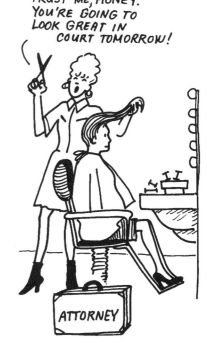

TRUST ME, HONEY.
YOU'RE GOING TO
LOOK GREAT IN
COURT TOMORROW!

ATTORNEY

_____

_____

_____

_____

_____   _____   _____

_____   _____   _____

_____   _____   _____

_____   _____   _____

_____   _____   _____

_____   _____   _____

_____   _____   _____

Name

Basic Skills/Spelling 6-8+

WORDS ON THE MOVE

One of the wonderful things about words is that you can use them to tell about **doing** so many things. Active words are very interesting and colorful to use, so you need to know how to spell them. Here are a few active words to practice spelling. All these words name some kind of action. And, oh, by the way, you'll have to unscramble them to get them spelled right.

1. gligew _____

2. fliroc _____

3. plogal _____

4. leprop _____

5. noubec _____

6. plrow _____

7. gargest _____

8. pramsec _____

9. duele _____

10. naermeuv _____

11. blowbe _____

12. revish _____

13. clutufate _____

14. trotae _____

15. blmic _____

16. dhurel _____

17. rursyc _____

18. klast _____

19. dlutner _____

20. naperc _____

21. lwarc _____

22. leef _____

23. surupe _____

24. dawdel _____

25. ptoms _____

Name _____

FEAST ON THESE

Don't get these words wrong, or it might spoil their flavor. Write the correct words in the "Gourmet Delights" section. Find the incorrect words, and write them correctly in the "Delectable Entrees" section.

GOURMET DELIGHTS COOK BOOK

carmel **caulaflour**

CANTALOPE **biscets**

soufflé CUSTERD

barbeq chicken **cinnamon**

chilly *apacado*

cucumber brocoli

COCOA tortilla **sunday** **lettuse**

moka *casserole* **éclair** **croisant** CHOCOLATE

omalet

DELECTABLE ENTREES COOK BOOK

tempura ketchup

Spaghetti sourkraut

lasana BURRITO

PRETZLE

Name _____

CHARACTERISTICALLY SPEAKING

Do you like to be around **obstreperous** people? Or do you prefer a **fastidious** friend? (You might need to look these words up to answer the questions!) The word-parts below can form words which describe characteristics of people. Put them together to correctly spell thirty characteristics. Choose one of the endings for each beginning. Some endings will be used more than once. Decide whether each word describes a characteristic you would like in a friend. Next to each one, write **yes** or **no**.

```
                TIOUS                    ER

   ORN              iOUS       LY    ANT

   LESS      aL    ive              ic    iLe

   iNG            SOME               Y
                           eD

   aBLe    iaR       OUS          ite
```

1.	fastid	11.	sur	21.	witt
2.	defi	12.	touch	22.	letharg
3.	abras	13.	agree	23.	imaginat
4.	pol	14.	errat	24.	clev
5.	creat	15.	pecul	25.	entertain
6.	cau	16.	stubb	26.	bor
7.	negat	17.	grouch	27.	jeal
8.	critic	18.	host	28.	bigot
9.	adventur	19.	vigor	29.	toler
10.	reclus	20.	rest	30.	secret

PEOPLE CAN REALLY BE CHARACTERS

Name

A LETTER OF QUALITY

Quaint, quick, quizzical, and quite quirky! **Q** lends a unique sparkle to a word, whether it's found at the beginning, middle, or near the end. In many word games, **Q** gets more points than most other letters.

Give the correct spelling of a **Q** word that fits each description below. (The first letter of each word is given.)

AFTER A REQUEST FROM THE CLASS QUIDNUNC,* I'VE QUADRUPLED OUR QUOTA OF QUIZZES!

SPELLING QUIZ TODAY

1. get to know   a _____

2. often   f _____

3. a review of an artistic work   c _____

4. another chapter to the story   s _____

5. an exclusive group   c _____

6. find "not guilty"   a _____

7. great spread of food   b _____

8. sufficient quantity   a _____

9. to take over   c _____

10. deposits that collect on teeth   p _____

11. unusual   u _____

12. results of actions   c _____

13. failing to uphold obligations   d _____

14. argument   q _____

15. hideous   g _____

16. no light passes through   o _____

17. varnish   l _____

18. pretend   m _____

* a "know-it-all"

Name _____

FROM SACRED TO SASSAFRAS

S starts off superb words such as sassafras, superior, soufflé, and smithereens. **S** words are some of the most common words in the English language. Practice spelling these commonly used **S** words that sometimes stump spellers. Do this by writing ten sentences—each having at least four of these **S** words in them. Make sure you spell the words correctly. You might try to write a sentence which has ALL **S** words.

SACRED

stew
sedative
shears
shriek
shrewd
situation
sinister
stagger
suspicious
solemn
scared
sacred
shush
stalk
stationery
surround
soprano
stethoscope
surgeon
sturgeon
syrup
significant
striped
squander
summit
secretive
severe
sneer

solo
synonym
surplus
soufflé
strudel
somersault
soccer
sacred
secretary
stallion
shoulder
soothe
sherbet
sauerkraut
subsequent
sympathy
splendid
security
smooth
spontaneous
supersonic
surfboard
section
scowl
surplus
suburban
survival
stereophonic

SASSAFRAS

Name _____

THE TROUBLE WITH W

The trouble with **W** is that so many words which start with it sound alike. Which . . . witch . . . whether . . . weather . . . wither . . . wherever . . . when . . . where . . . wherefore . . . .why . . . what . . . and so on. You really have to know the differences between your **W** words to spell them correctly. Correct any **W** words that are spelled wrong in these sentences. Just cross out the words, and write the correct spelling above them.

1. Reched wether always seems to welcum us whin we arrive in the wildernes for our weakly campout.

2. "Stop wining!," I wisper to my sister, as I waver and woble, struggling to carry her wait.

WILD AND WACKY
WEATHER THIS WEEKEND

3. Whover took my rench? Are there any witneses to this theft wich must have just happened?

4. We wernt writting words of whisdom that day wile we wandered along the path in that wierd school writting activity. Actually we wernt wholy paying attention.

5. I'm woried about the weezing cough my sister Winnie has had ever since we swam by the wirlpool.

6. Rinkled clothes, wiked jokes, and waistful habits may lead adults to think you are withhout whisdom or good sense.

7. Her great whit is her best wepon against her whithering shyness.

8. I'm not sure weather or not you can help us make wreeths, as that is the worstest wreeth I ever saw.

9. Ware did you get that wreched pair of pants hanging around your waste? Whos are those wierd things? They make you look as if you way an extra fifty pounds.

10. Hopefully, widespred advertising will bring a large group of wimin to the meeting on Wensday.

Name _____

X-CEPTIONAL WORDS

You might think of "X-rated" when you hear about **X**. But actually, most words with **X** in them are NOT **X**-rated! Just interesting. And sometimes **X**-ceptional. Below are the meanings of some words that have the letter **X** in them. Write each word—being careful to get the **X** in the right place and, of course, to spell the whole word correctly.

1. e **X** _____ (a species that is no longer living)

2. a **X** _____ (Earth rotates on it)

3. e **X** _____ (stretch the truth)

4. e **X** _____ (look at carefully)

5. o _____ **X** (strictly adhere to rules)

6. c _____ **X** (complicated)

7. e **X** _____ (very expensive)

8. e **X** _____ (excused from the rules)

9. e **X** _____ (stir up, incite)

10. e **X** _____ (breathe out)

11. e **X** _____ (reason for not doing something)

12. e **X** _____ (dig up)

13. r _____ **X** (instinctive reaction)

14. e **X** _____ (pull out)

15. ma **X** _____ (not minimum)

16. e **X** _____ (too much)

17. c _____ **X** _____ (condition of skin)

18. e **X** _____ d (disgusted)

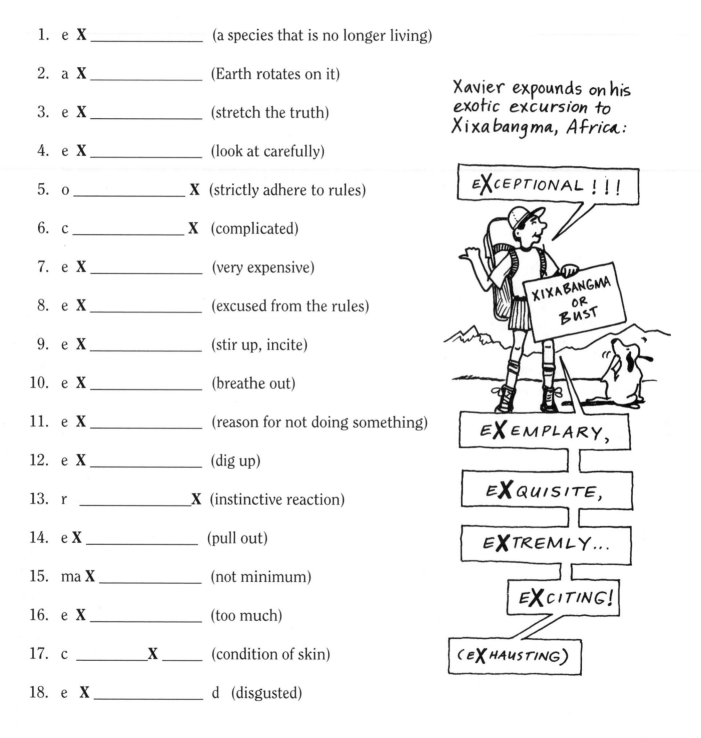

Xavier expounds on his exotic excursion to Xixabangma, Africa:

EXCEPTIONAL ! ! !

XIXABANGMA OR BUST

EXEMPLARY,

EXQUISITE,

EXTREMLY...

EXCITING!

(EXHAUSTING)

Name _____

Y NOT?

Sometimes it's hard to remember just whether or not a word has a Y. Sometimes it's hard to remember exactly where to put the Y. Why not practice these common Y words, so you won't wonder? The words are scrambled, but there's a clue to help you figure out what they are. Unscramble them and write them correctly.

1. yocnev   carry something somewhere   _____

2. amytnno   a word that's opposite   _____

3. connay   a river flows through it   _____

4. cybilec   something to ride   _____

5. nymonys   word meaning the same   _____

6. yenv   jealousy   _____

7. thym   fictional story   _____

8. fedy   stand up to or oppose   _____

9. thymrh   musical beat   _____

10. omunnysua   no name given   _____

11. mehyr   poetry does it   _____

12. stymmsop   tells if you're sick   _____

13. pycano   an overhead cover   _____

14. phesisyhot   scientific theory   _____

15. arassipyl   inability to move   _____

16. fytimys   to puzzle   _____

17. phayta   no energy   _____

18. whcey   exercises your jaw   _____

Name _____

Z LAST WORD

Which words have it? **Z** gets thrown into words where it doesn't belong. Sometimes we hear a **Z** sound, but the spelling is an **S**. And when **Z** really is there—are there one or two? Complete the puzzle below using correctly spelled words that have **Z** in them. In all cases, the **Z** is not at the beginning of the word.

Down

1. a fashion fad
2. to put in danger
5. a cutting tool
7. to become aware of
9. layer of the atmosphere
10. picture it in your mind
11. to demolish
13. blinding snowstorm
15. to put into words
17. sharp-edged tool
18. mesmerize
22. skin eruptions

Across

3. a danger
4. to take by force
6. a reward
8. to say you're sorry
12. to convert into ions
14. questioning
16. south seas blue
18. smog
19. snug
20. Indian corn
21. a lovers' meeting
23. indolence
24. carcass-eater

Name

LAUGHABLE WORDS

Spelling, of course, is no laughing matter. But there are words about laughing and words to make you laugh. Actually, *laugh* is kind of a funny word to begin with. It isn't spelled the way it sounds. And it's not the sound that comes out when you do laugh. This makes it a little tricky to spell. Other words about laughing are sometimes spelling hazards too. Each of these twenty-four words has something to do with laughter. Enough letters are given to help you figure out what the words are and to help you spell them correctly.

1. l a ___ ___ ___

2. l a ___ ___ ___ ___ b l e

3. l a ___ ___ ___ ___ e r

4. a m u ___ ___ ___ ___ n t

5. c o ___ ___ my

6. c o m ___ ___ ___ a n

7. c o ___ ___ c

8. ___ ___ gg ___ e

9. c h ___ ___ ___ le

10. m ___ ___ th

11. h ___ ___ ar ___ ___ ___ s

12. j ___ ___ ___

13. h ___ ___ or ___ ___ s

14. h ___ ___ ___ r

15. m ___ rr ___ ___ ___ nt

16. w ___ tt ___

17. a m ___ ___ ing

18. w ___ ___ ___ cr ___ ___ ___

19. mis ___ ___ ___ ___ f

20. b ___ ff ___ ___ n

21. r ___ ___ ___ cule

22. pr ___ ___ ___ ster

23. lud ___ ___ ___ ___ ___ ___

24. am ___ ___ e

I'M A JOKESTER,
A CLOWN
A PUNSTER
A TWIT,
A SIDE-SPLITTING
JESTER,
A COMIC –
A WIT!

YOU MAY SNICKER,
OR DOUBLE IN HALF,
BUT I'M THE
COMEDIAN
WHO MADE YOU
LAUGH!

GAG BAG

Name

Basic Skills/Spelling 6-8+

EMPHATICALLY SPEAKING!

Oh, no! These emphatic statements are all plagued with spelling errors. Fix them! Quickly!
Cross out the errors, and write the correctly spelled words underneath.

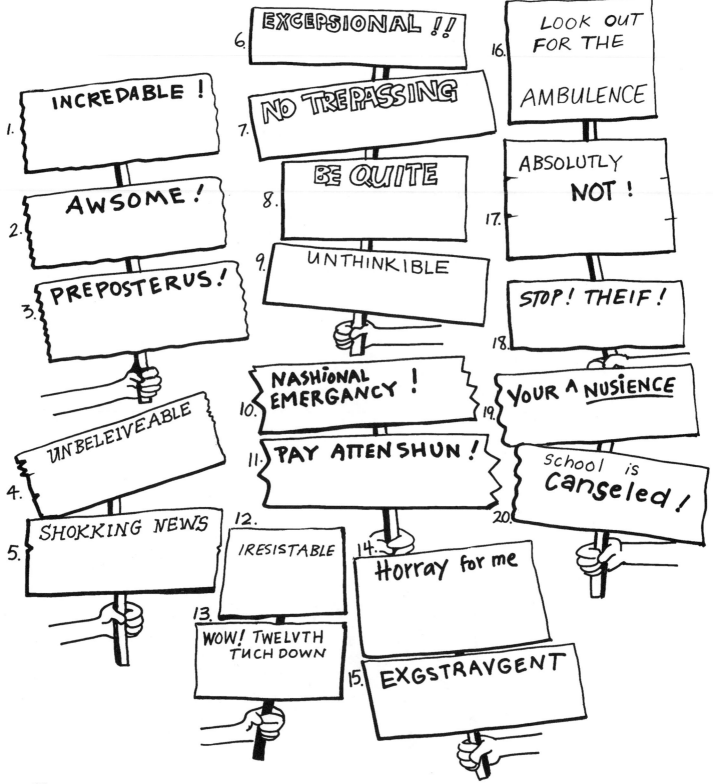

6. EXCEPSIONAL !!

16. LOOK OUT FOR THE AMBULENCE

1. INCREDABLE !

7. NO TREPASSING

8. BE QUITE

17. ABSOLUTLY NOT !

2. AWSOME !

9. UNTHINKIBLE

18. STOP! THEIF !

3. PREPOSTERUS !

10. NASHIONAL EMERGANCY !

19. YOUR A NUSIENCE

4. UNBELEIVEABLE

11. PAY ATTENSHUN !

20. School is Canseled !

5. SHOKKING NEWS

12. IRESISTABLE

14. Horray for me

13. WOW! TWELVTH TUCH DOWN

15. EXGSTRAVGENT

Name

HELP NEEDED!

You may not be able to help the situation described in the letter. But you can help with the spelling. Correct each misspelled word in Serena's letter by writing it above the wrong word.

Febuary 6

Dear Abby,

I'm sorry you missed the show. Finally I have time to tell you abot it.

It was an akward trick for a gorrilla, I admit, to clim onto a trapeeze balincing an arkatect and an artachoke on oppisite arms. Fortunatly, we hired a talanted gorrilla. This may seen wierd—not your obveous cercus preformence. But you have to admit, it was a unick idea. And certen peple flocked to perchase expenseve tickets.

The gorrilla was a tame and calm one, with no obveous tendancies toward vilence. He had practised this trick many times, even preforming it at a bankquet before a group of famos polatitians.

As the curtin went up and the show began, I was greatful that everything was going smoothely. And then—there was the mosquitoe that somhow got onto the gorrilla's tonge. Are freindly pet turned feirce. In less than a minit, he swung down to the net, turned a huge sommersalt, and devored the archatect—hole, as an unbeleving croud of spectaters, including me, wached in horor.

Sorry you missed it.

Your friend,
Serena

SPECIAL EDITION
TRAGEDY AT BIG-TOP
APE EATS FELLOW

ERRONEOUS HEADLINES

News writer needs spelling lessons! Editors requested! These headlines need a good copy editor. Find and fix the errors in all the headlines below.

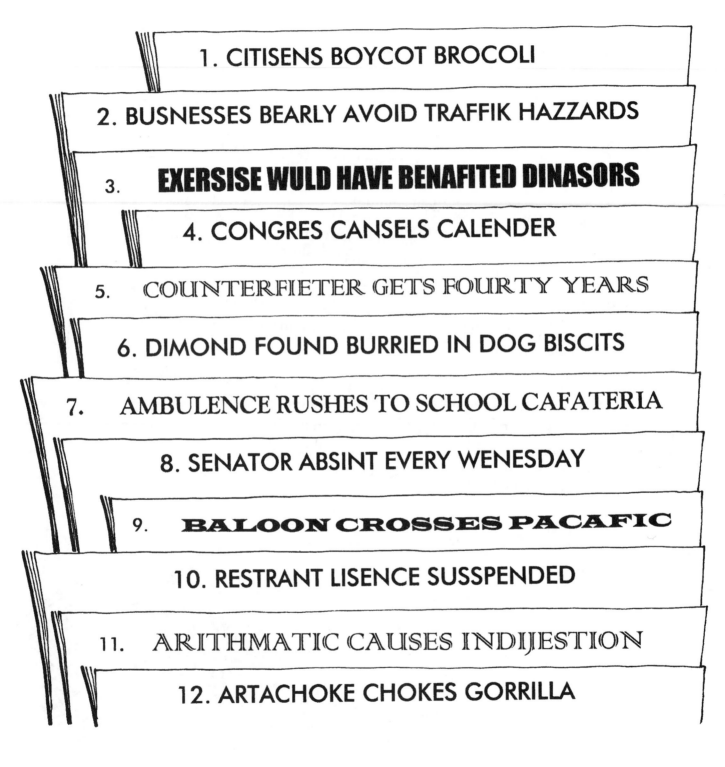

1. CITISENS BOYCOT BROCOLI

2. BUSNESSES BEARLY AVOID TRAFFIK HAZZARDS

3. EXERSISE WULD HAVE BENAFITED DINASORS

4. CONGRES CANSELS CALENDER

5. COUNTERFIETER GETS FOURTY YEARS

6. DIMOND FOUND BURRIED IN DOG BISCITS

7. AMBULENCE RUSHES TO SCHOOL CAFATERIA

8. SENATOR ABSINT EVERY WENESDAY

9. BALOON CROSSES PACAFIC

10. RESTRANT LISENCE SUSSPENDED

11. ARITHMATIC CAUSES INDIJESTION

12. ARTACHOKE CHOKES GORRILLA

Name

APPENDIX

CONTENTS

300+ COMMONLY MISSPELLED WORDS

absence	breakfast	desert	height
accident	breath (n.)	diamond	here
account	breathe (v.)	difference	history
accurate	brief	doctor	hoarse
accuse	built	does	hour
ache	bureau	done	hypothesis
achieve	burglar	don't	icicle
architect	business	early	ignorance
acre	busy	easy	immature
address	buy	education	immediately
adolescent	cafeteria	efficiency	improvement
advertise	canal	embarrass	incident
again	cannot	empty	independence
aisle	canoe	enough	infection
allowance	can't	every	influence
already	capacity	exhaust	initial
always	carburetor	explain	innocent
amateur	carton	extraordinary	interrupt
ambulance	cashier	fatigue	interview
among	caught	February	irregular
ancient	certain	forget	island
angel	character	forty	instead
anniversary	chief	fountain	jealous
anonymous	choose	fourth	jeopardy
answer	chorus	fragile	journal
anxious	climb	frequent	journey
any	cocoa	friend	juice
August	collar	frighten	just
baking	color	gauge	justice
balloon	Columbus	genius	kitchen
beauty	coming	ghost	knead
beautiful	committee	gnaw	knew
because	cough	gorgeous	knife
been	could	graduate	knives
beginning	country	grammar	knock
believe	courage	grief	know
benefit	courtesy	guarantee	laboratory
bicycle	damage	guess	laid
biscuit	dear	half	language
blizzard	deceive	having	lawyer
blue	defense	hear	league
brake	deficient	heaven	legislature
break	delicious	heard	library

Basic Skills/Spelling 6-8+

Copyright ©1997 by Incentive Publications, Inc., Nashville, TN.

librarian	occurrence	recognize	typical
lieutenant	official	refer	unconscious
lightning	often	rehearse	uniform
likable	once	reign	unique
likeness	opaque	remedy	united
limousine	opportunity	require	universe
Lincoln	opposite	reservoir	unusual
literature	ordinary	resign	usable
location	original	rhythm	used
loose	ought	ridiculous	usually
lose	outrageous	said	vacuum
machinery	pajamas	says	vegetable
magnify	particle	scene	vehicle
making	paid	seems	very
manageable	parallel	seize	villain
many	parliament	separate	virtue
marriage	peculiar	shoes	virus
marshmallow	people	since	visible
meant	perform	sincere	voice
measurement	physician	sleigh	waist
medal	picnic	society	waste
medium	piece	some	wear
memorize	pilot	stalk	weather
miscellaneous	pleasant	straight	Wednesday
minute	pleasure	sugar	week
molecule	pledge	sure	weigh
mortgage	police	taught	where
mosquito	politics	tear	whether
movement	presence	technique	which
much	program	terrific	whoever
national	protein	their	whole
naughty	quantity	they	women
necessary	quaint	thorough	won't
negligence	quarrel	though	would
neighbor	quarter	through	wreath
neither	question	tired	write
none	quiet	tonight	writhe
noticeable	quite	tongue	writing
nuclear	quotient	too	wrote
nuisance	raise	triangle	yellow
numb	read	trouble	yolk
obey	ready	truly	your
occasionally	realize	Tuesday	you're
occur	recent	two	zipper

WORDS THAT CONFUSE

accept (receive) — **except** (exclude)

ad hoc (temporary) — **ad lib** (unrehearsed remark)

advice (recommendation) — **advise** (give advice)

affect (to influence) — **effect** (result)

all together (all in a group) — **altogether** (completely)

allude (refer to) — **elude** (to escape)

allusion (an indirect reference) — **illusion** (a false impression)

anxious (uneasy) — **eager** (to be enthusiastic)

astrology (telling the future by the stars) — **astronomy** (the study of planets and stars)

avenge (to get justice) — **revenge** (retaliation to get even)

censor (someone who prohibits something) — **censure** (to criticize)

cite (to refer to) — **quote** (to repeat precisely)

clench (to grip tightly) — **clinch** (to fasten together)

complacent (showing satisfaction) — **compliant** (submissive)

confidant (someone you tell secrets to) — **confident** (certain, sure)

connote (to suggest another meaning) — **denote** (to express clearly)

credulous (gullible, will believe anything) — **credible** (believable)

diagnosis (identifying the problem) — **prognosis** (predicting what to expect)

diffuse (to spread out) — **defuse** (to lower or end an explosive situation)

elicit (to obtain information) — **illicit** (illegal)

elegy (a funeral song or poem) — **eulogy** (words of praise spoken at a funeral)

equinox (time that day & night are same length) — **solstice** (longest & shortest days of the year)

epic (a long narrative poem about a hero) — **saga** (a story with many scenes)

exception (removed from a usual expectation) — **exemption** (to excuse from obligation)

explicit (clearly stated) — **implicit** (suggested but not stated clearly)

flaunt (show off) — **flout** (openly disregard)

immigrant (one who has gone to a new country) — **migrant** (one who moves from place to place)

imminent (near at hand) — **eminent** (prominent, high in ability)

imply (suggest) — **infer** (draw conclusions based on information)

incandescent (intensely bright and clear) — **iridescent** (shimmering with rainbow color)

legato (music with smooth sound) — **staccato** (disjointed, choppy music)

libel (to publish damaging information) — **slander** (to say false things about someone)

loath (unwilling) — **loathe** (to detest)

majority (more than half) — **plurality** (the highest number of votes)

martinet (severe disciplinarian) — **marionette** (a puppet operated by strings)

metaphor (suggested comparison of two dissimilar things) — **simile** (comparison of two dissimilar things using *like* or *as*)

momentous (very important) — **monumental** (large and long-lasting)

monotheism (belief in one god) — **polytheism** (belief in more than one god)

nadir (lowest point) — **zenith** (highest point)

nefarious (wicked) — **notorious** (famous)

oblige (feel a debt of gratitude) — **obligate** (compelled to do something)

oral (spoken language) — **verbal** (written or spoken language)

palate (sense of taste) — **palette** (range of colors used by an artist)

perennial (continuing longer than a year) — **annual** (once yearly)

perpetrate (carry out) — **perpetuate** (preserve or prolong)

persecute (to harass) — **prosecute** (to start legal action against)

precipitate (to hurl downward) — **precipitous** (extremely steep)

prerequisite (required beforehand) — **requisite** (required)

prescribe (to order or suggest) — **proscribe** (to disallow)

quarrelsome (argumentative) — **querulous** (complaining a lot)

rebuff (snub or beat back) — **rebut** (prove something wrong)

repel (drive off) — **repulse** (reject by being unkind)

restive (restless or uneasy) — **restful** (providing relaxation)

reticent (not inclined to speak about) — **reluctant** (unwilling)

rigorous (strict or severe) — **vigorous** (full of energy)

rogue (a dishonest, mischievous person) — **villain** (an evil person)

shun (avoid or keep away from) — **spurn** (to reject with disdain)

specious (appearing to be good until you get a closer look) — **spurious** (false)

stump (to puzzle) — **stymie** (to block progress)

sumptuous (expensive and luxurious) — **scrumptious** (delicious)

tortuous (winding and twisting) — **torturous** (very painful)

transient (short term) — **transitory** (temporary)

tumultuous (noisy and disorderly) — **turbulent** (agitated)

veracious (truthful) — **voracious** (ravenous hunger)

wangle (to contrive or accomplish by cleverness) — **wrangle** (an angry argument)

wax (to increase in strength) — **wane** (to decrease in strength)

SPELLING RULES

Rule 1: Write **i** before **e** except after **c**, or when sounded like **a** as in **neighbor** and **weigh**. Some exceptions are: **their, height, foreign, heir, neither, weird,** and **seize.**

Rule 2: When a one-syllable word (**bat**) ends in a consonant (ba**t**) preceded by one vowel (b**a**t), double the final consonant before adding a suffix which begins with a vowel (ba**tt**ing). When a multisyllablic word (**for • get**) ends in a consonant (**t**), preceded by one vowel (**e**), the accent is on the last syllable (for**get**). If, in addition, the suffix begins with a vowel (**ing**)—the same rule holds true: Double the final consonant (forge**tt**ing; begi**nn**ing).

Rule 3: If a word ends with a silent **e**, drop the **e** before adding a suffix which begins with a vowel (use-using-useful; state-stating-statement; like-liking-likeness).
*Note: Do not drop the **e** when the suffix begins with a consonant. Exceptions include **truly, argument,** and **ninth.***

Rule 4: When **y** is the last letter in a word and the **y** comes just after a vowel, add **s** (toy-toys; play-plays; donkey-donkeys).

Rule 5: The word ending pronounced **shun** is usually spelled **tion.**

Rule 6: The spelling of a base word does not change when you add a prefix.

Rule 7: If the letter before a final **y** is a vowel, do not change the **y** when you add a suffix. If the letter before the final **y** is a consonant, change the **y** to **i** before you add any suffix except **ing.** The **y** never changes before **ing.**

Rule 8: When the letters **c** and **g** have a hard sound, they will be followed by **a, o,** or **u.** When they have a soft sound, they will be followed by the letters **i, e,** or **y.** Suffixes that follow the soft **c** or **g** will always begin with an **i** or **e: ian, ion, ious, ence.**

Rule 9: The letter **q** is always followed by the letter **u** in the English language.

Rule 10: The letters **gh** are silent in a few familiar letter combinations: **ough, ight, eigh.**

SPELLING
SKILLS TEST

Each question is worth 1 point. Total possible score: 100 points.

*For questions 1-10, choose **ie** or **ei** to correctly spell each word.*

1. ch_____f   6. ach ____ve

2. n ___ghbor   7. rec____ve

3. for____gn   8. quot ___nt

4. n____ther   9. w_____rd

5. w_____gh   10. s _____ze

For questions 11-28, choose the ending that correctly completes each word.

11. apolog_____(ise, ize, ice)

12. prom _____(ise, ice, is)

13. host_____(ige, age, ege)

14. marvel _____(us, ous, eous)

15. telev _____(ise, ize, ice)

16. tradi _____(tion, sion, cian)

17. danger _____(us, ous, eous)

18. contag ____(eous, ous, ious)

19. evid_____(ance, ense, ence)

20. sens _____(ible, able, eable)

21. vac _____(ant, ent, int)

22. cand _____(al, el, le, il)

23. fat_____(el, al, le, il)

24. signific_____(ent, ant, int)

25. wrest _____(el, al, le)

26. revers_____(ible, able, eable)

27. decor _____(eat, ate, at)

28. icic _____(il, al, el, le)

For questions 29-38, if a word has one or more silent letters, write the letters. If a word has no silent letters, write NO.

_____ 29. empathy

_____ 30. gnu

_____ 31. judge

_____ 32. answer

_____ 33. memory

_____ 34. resignation

_____ 35. sword

_____ 36. stalk

_____ 37. pride

_____ 38. benefit

For questions 39-43, add a prefix to make a word that fits the meaning given.

_____ 39. approved (not approved)

_____ 40. ordinary (beyond ordinary)

_____ 41. regular (not regular)

_____ 42. state (between states)

_____ 43. germ (against germs)

For questions 44-48, add a root to make a word that fits the meaning given.

_____ 44. ility (ability to move)

_____ 45. ible (able to be touched)

_____ 46. ify (to show to be truthful)

_____ 47. ant (to be in a state of sleep)

_____ 48. inous (to be full of light)

For questions 49-58, choose the correct word to complete the sentence. Write the word on the line.

49. _____
The (principal, principle) manages the school.

50. _____
A concrete wall is a (stationary, stationery) object.

51. _____
Three frightening (incidence, incidents) happened to me today.

52. _____
We visited the (capital, capitol) building of our state.

53. _____
Everything's okay (accept, except) my two broken legs.

54. _____
Your rude behavior doesn't (effect, affect) me in the least.

55. _____
I've got some good (advise, advice) for you about romance.

56. _____
I'll tell you, (weather, whether) or not you want to hear.

57. _____
Do you know what obtuse (angles, angels) are?

58. _____
I did a (through, though, thorough) job of cleaning my room.

Name _____

Basic Skills/Spelling 6-8+

For questions 59-69, correct the spelling of these misspelled words. Write each word on the line.

_____ 59. Lincon

_____ 60. doller

_____ 61. twoard

_____ 62. Conneticut

_____ 63. oppossum

_____ 64. pharmicist

_____ 65. manuver

_____ 66. choclate

_____ 67. Republacan

_____ 68. Pilgrums

_____ 69. peculier

For questions 70-78, write the correct spelling on the line.

_____ 70. butiful, beautuful, beautiful

_____ 71. busness, business, buisness

_____ 72. receive, recieve, receave

_____ 73. baloon, ballon, balloon

_____ 74. separate, seperate, sepurate

_____ 75. enough, enuogh, enuf

_____ 76. occurred, occured, ocurred

_____ 77. advertisement, advertizement, advertisment

_____ 78. benifit, benefit, benafit

For questions 79-85, correct the spelling of these misspelled words. Write the word on the line.

_____ 79. exsitement

_____ 80. suspisious

_____ 81. apologise

_____ 82. exeption

_____ 83. amuzement

_____ 84. exagerate

_____ 85. suprize

For questions 86-90, rewrite each misspelled word correctly.

86. Was there inadaquat food at the Big Eater's banquite? _____

_____

87. Did Colombus realy descover Amerika?

_____

_____

88. How long did it take the libarians to travel from San Fransisco to Los Angelas?

_____

_____

89. The docter won't give you an excuze from skool if you don't have eny symtoms of ilness.

_____

_____

_____

90. Is an antomim oppisit from a synanym?

_____

_____

For questions 91-100, choose the correct spelling for each word. Write it on the line.

_____ 91. resturant, restaurant, reasturant

_____ 92. celender, calander, calendar

_____ 93. embarrass, embarass, embarras

_____ 94. hippopotamas, hippopotomas, hippopotamus

_____ 95. lisence, lisense, license

_____ 96. necessary, nesesary, necesary

_____ 97. laborotory, labratory, laboratory

_____ 98. noticeable, noticible, noticable

_____ 99. dinasaur, dinosaur, dinosoar

_____ 100. paralel, parralel, parallel

SCORE: Total Points _____ out of a possible 100 points

Name _____

SPELLING
SKILLS TEST ANSWER KEY

1. ie (chief)
2. ei (neighbor)
3. ei (foreign)
4. ei (neither)
5. ei (weigh)
6. ie (achieve)
7. ei (receive)
8. ie (quotient)
9. ei (weird)
10. ei (seize)
11. ize (apologize)
12. ise (promise)
13. age (hostage)
14. ous (marvelous)
15. ise (televise)
16. tion (tradition)
17. ous (dangerous)
18. ious (contagious)
19. ence (evidence)
20. ible (sensible)
21. ant (vacant)
22. le (candle)
23. al (fatal)
24. ant (significant)
25. le (wrestle)
26. ible (reversible)
27. ate (decorate)
28. le (icicle)
29. no
30. g
31. d
32. w
33. no
34. no
35. w

36. l
37. e
38. no
39. dis (disapproved)
40. extra (extraordinary)
41. ir (irregular)
42. inter (interstate)
43. anti (antigerm)
44. mob (mobility)
45. tang (tangible)
46. ver (verify)
47. dorm (dormant)
48. lum (luminous)
49. principal
50. stationary
51. incidents
52. capitol
53. except
54. affect
55. advice
56. whether
57. angles
58. thorough
59. Lincoln
60. dollar
61. toward
62. Connecticut
63. opossum
64. pharmacist
65. maneuver
66. chocolate
67. Republican
68. Pilgrims
69. peculiar
70. beautiful

71. business
72. receive
73. balloon
74. separate
75. enough
76. occurred
77. advertisement
78. benefit
79. excitement
80. suspicious
81. apologize
82. exception
83. amusement
84. exaggerate
85. surprise
86. inadequate; banquet
87. Columbus; really; discover; America
88. librarians; San Francisco; Los Angeles
89. doctor; excuse; school; any; symptoms; illness
90. antonym; opposite; synonym
91. restaurant
92. calendar
93. embarrass
94. hippopotamus
95. license
96. necessary
97. laboratory
98. noticeable
99. dinosaur
100. parallel

ANSWERS

page 10

List 1
Incorrect
2, 7, 10, 11, 12, 13, 14, 15, 17, 19, 22, 24, 25

List 2
Incorrect
1, 3, 4, 5, 6, 8, 9, 16, 18, 20, 21, 23

page 11

1. dilemma
2. arithmetic
3. different
4. cafeteria
5. calendar
6. college
7. anonymous
8. excess
9. criticize
10. necessary
11. vegetables
12. recognize
13. laughter
14. August
15. through

page 12

1. okay
2. okay
3. benefit
4. okay
5. okay
6. animal
7. okay
8. omitted
9. embarrass
10. okay
11. quizzical
12. okay
13. okay
14. bazaar
15. cereal
16. okay
17. ammonia
18. traveling
19. okay
20. parallel
21. okay
22. okay
23. ballot
24. barracuda
25. balcony
26. okay
27. okay
28. okay
29. okay
30. memory
31. okay
32. opossum
33. hippopotamus
34. staccato
35. Tennessee
36. okay
37. centennial
38. okay
39. professor
40. celebrate

page 13

1. freight
2. sleigh
3. neighborhood
4. mischief
5. achieve
6. reign
7. conscience
8. conceited
9. quotient
10. piece
11. society
12. efficient
13. grief
14. science
15. eight
16. weight
17. deficient
18. convenient
19. hygiene
20. shriek

page 14

1. B   15. C
2. C   16. B
3. B   17. A
4. C   18. C
5. B   19. B
6. C   20. B
7. B   21. C
8. A   22. A
9. C   23. B
10. B   24. C
11. C   25. C
12. C   26. We don't
13. C   stick with
14. C   these rules.

page 15

1. motto
2. forgot
3. cocoon
4. odor
5. common
6. monsoon
7. photograph
8. toxicology
9. foolproof
10. follow
11. logo
12. tattoo
13. overlook
14. loon
15. locomotive
16. kazoo
17. orator
18. monocle
19. porous
20. voodoo
21. scorpion
22. opponent
23. sophomore
24. monotonous

page 16

Below are some suggested answers. Consider any answer that makes sense and contains a silent letter.

1. Ghetto
2. Dough
3. Gnaws
4. Crumbs
5. Gnu
6. Wrapped
7. Judge; Bridge
8. Answers
9. Resigns
10. Knight; Sword
11. Raspberries
12. Ptomaine
13. Knife
14. Dumb
15. Pledge
16. Stalked
17. Badge
18. Lambs
19. Knock
20. Reigns

page 17

1. ph
2. ph
3. ph
4. gh
5. ph
6. gh
7. ph
8. gh
9. ph
10. gh
11. ph
12. ph
13. gh
14. ph
15. ph
16. ph
17. gh
18. ph; ph

page 18

1. prescription
2. exclude
3. rewrite
4. conform
5. depart
6. subdivide
7. translate
8. microchip
9. prolong
10. invisible
11. advance
12. bibliography
13. extraordinary
14. ultrasonic
15. disapprove
16. tricycle
17. antiwar
18. untied

page 19

1. verify
2. altitude
3. empathy
4. tangible
5. pacifist
6. durable
7. librarian
8. mobility
9. population
10. suspend
11. fracture
12. transfer
13. dormant
14. autobiography
15. action
16. journal
17. luminous
18. astrology
19. ridiculous
20. biography

page 20

1. distant
2. important
3. vacant
4. restaurant
5. elephant
6. pleasant
7. significant
8. defiant
9. elegant
10. applicant
11. observant
12. vigilant
13. occupant

Basic Skills/Spelling 6-8+

14. ignorant
15. assistant
16. defendant
17. hydrant
18. contestant
19. constant
20. inhabitants

page 21

1. ate
2. ate
3. ate
4. eat
5. ate
6. ate
7. eat
8. ate
9. eat
10. eat
11. ate
12. ate
13. eat
14. ate
15. ate
16. ate
17. ate
18. eat
19. ate
20. ate
21. ate
22. ate
23. eat
24. ate
25. ate
26. eat

page 22

1. frugal
2. hysterical
3. candle
4. principal or principle
5. ok
6. ok
7. gargle
8. ok
9. angel or angle
10. ok
11. ok
12. ok
13. unravel
14. legal
15. wrestle
16. spiral
17. clavicle
18. ok
19. vessel
20. ok
21. channel
22. ok
23. visible
24. radical
25. ok
26. ok

27. ok
28. obstacle
29. ok
30. travel
31. ok
32. carnival

page 23

1. ize
2. ile
3. ile
4. ive
5. ish
6. ise
7. ism or ize
8. ish
9. ish
10. ive
11. ive
12. ist or ism
13. ile
14. ish
15. ite or ish
16. ish
17. ive
18. ism or ize
19. ise
20. ive
21. ism
22. ist
23. ish
24. ize
25. ist, ism, or ize
26. ize
27. ite
28. ist
29. ist

page 24

1. tion
2. tion
3. cian
4. sion
5. sion
6. sion
7. tion
8. tion
9. ion
10. tion
11. cian
12. tune
13. ous
14. ous
15. ous
16. us
17. ious
18. eous
19. us
20. ius
21. us
22. ious
23. ous
24. uous

page 25

1. ence
2. ence
3. ance
4. ence
5. ence
6. ence
7. ance
8. ance
9. ence
10. ance
11. ence
12. ence
13. ance
14. ance
15. ence
16. ible
17. ible
18. able
19. able
20. ible
21. ible
22. able
23. able
24. ible
25. ible
26. able
27. ible
28. able
29. able
30. ible

page 26

1. anguish
2. chaos
3. treacherous
4. fraud
5. pauper
6. drought
7. cougar
8. thesaurus
9. bias
10. boisterous
11. camouflage
12. plausible
13. eloquent
14. aquarium
15. sausage
16. beard
17. leopard
18. cauliflower
19. influenza
20. against
21. thought
22. disguise

page 27

1. minor
2. scared; sacred
3. sword; heir
4. principal; incidents; incidence; dessert

5. pedal; pedal
6. peer; pier
7. soared; desert; miner
8. capital; capitol; hair
9. Altogether
10. stationery

page 28

Answers will vary.

page 29

1. emerald
2. mosquito
3. macaroni
4. kindergarten
5. yacht; buoy
6. algebra; chemistry
7. antique
8. magazine
9. sauerkraut
10. paradise
11. gorilla; mosquito; mustang
12. sarong
13. veto
14. piano; tambourine

page 30

Answers will vary.

page 31

I. I always lose my notes when I get ready for a test, except for math, because I wrap my lunch in those and always have them near. My mother gives me unending advice about how to get through this problem, but, I assure you, it's a useless exercise. It'll be major coup if I ever get accepted into any college.

II.
1. through; through
2. whether; weather
3. prosecute
4. which
5. angel
6. commas
7. inflict
8. implied
9. incredible
10. extrovert

page 32

1. sacred
2. curse
3. earth
4. silent
5. terrain
6. dread
7. thing
8. icons
9. charm

10. gears
11. alter
12. lament
13. teach

page 33

1. about
2. above
3. ache
4. after
5. alike
6. almost
7. already
8. always
9. aren't
10. attach
11. awful
12. balance
13. bottle
14. bridge
15. bury
16. certain
17. chief
18. choice
19. collar
20. dairy
21. dollar
22. doubt
23. edge
24. enough
25. **correct**
26. forty
27. ghost
28. guess
29. hoping
30. island
31. juice
32. knock
33. laugh
34. length
35. lovely
36. obey
37. often
38. people
39. piece
40. probably
41. receive
42. raise
43. safety
44. sense
45. stomach
46. Tuesday
47. toward
48. useful
49. **correct**
50. when
51. whose

Page 34

Check to see that words are spelled correctly.

page 35

1. Albuquerque
2. Antarctica
3. August
4. Boise
5. Braille
6. Coca Cola®
7. Columbus
8. Connecticut
9. Declaration of Independence
10. Democrat
11. Des Moines
12. District of Columbia
13. Egypt
14. Eisenhower
15. February
16. Hiroshima
17. Hungary
18. Lincoln
19. Los Angeles
20. Massachusetts
21. Minnesota
22. Mediterranean
23. Nagasaki
24. Pacific
25. Panama Canal
26. Parliament
27. Pilgrims
28. Rio Grande
29. Republican
30. Romania
31. San Francisco
32. Statue of Liberty
33. Tallahassee
34. Tropic of Capricorn
35. Tuesday
36. Tyrannosaurus Rex
37. Vancouver
38. Venezuela
39. Wednesday
40. Zaire

page 36

1. barracuda
2. leopard
3. panther
4. elephant
5. giraffe
6. crocodile
7. coyote
8. vulture
9. termite
10. rhinoceros
11. dinosaur
12. chameleon
13. hippopotamus
14. orangutan
15. opossum
16. tarantula
17. scorpion
18. llama
19. zebra

Answer: a fancy name for a zoo

page 37

actor
actress
attorney
banker
beautician
butcher
carpenter
chef
comic
cook
dancer
electrician
financier
firefighter
grocer
judge
lifeguard
manager
mayor
mechanic
minister
musician
nurse
opthamologist
orthodontist
pharmacist
physicist
plumber
professor
senator
sculptor
singer
surgeon
teacher
waiter

page 38

1. wiggle
2. frolic
3. gallop
4. propel
5. bounce
6. prowl
7. stagger
8. scamper
9. elude
10. maneuver
11. wobble
12. shiver
13. fluctuate
14. rotate
15. climb
16. hurdle
17. scurry
18. stalk
19. trundle
20. prance
21. crawl
22. flee
23. pursue
24. waddle
25. stomp

page 39

CORRECT ("Delights")
soufflé
éclair
tortilla
spaghetti
cocoa
tempura
cucumber
casserole
ketchup
chocolate
cinnamon

INCORRECT ("Entrees")
cantaloupe
cauliflower
chili
broccoli
caramel
sundae
biscuits
custard
mocha
lettuce
barbecue chicken
croissant
pretzel
avocado
omelette or omelet
sauerkraut
lasagna

page 40

1. ious
2. ant
3. ive
4. ite
5. ive
6. tious
7. ive
8. al
9. ous
10. ive
11. ly
12. y
13. able
14. ic
15. iar
16. orn
17. y
18. ile
19. ous
20. less
21. y
22. ic
23. ive
24. er
25. ing
26. ing
27. ous
28. ed
29. ant
30. ive

page 41

1. acquaint
2. frequent
3. critique
4. sequel
5. clique
6. acquit
7. banquet
8. adequate
9. conquer
10. plaque
11. unique
12. consequences
13. delinquent
14. quarrel
15. grotesque
16. opaque
17. lacquer
18. masquerade

page 42

Answers will vary.

page 43

1. Wretched weather always seems to welcome us when we arrive in the wilderness for our weekly campout.
2. "Stop whining!" I whisper to my sister, as I waver and wobble, struggling to carry her weight.

3. Whoever took my wrench? Are there any witnesses to this theft which must have just happened?
4. We weren't writing words of wisdom that day while we wandered along the path in that weird school writing activity. Actually we weren't wholly paying attention.
5. I'm worried about the wheezing cough my sister Winnie has had ever since we swam by the whirlpool.
6. Wrinkled clothes, wicked jokes, and wasteful habits may lead adults to think you are without wisdom or good sense.
7. Her great wit is her best weapon against her withering shyness.
8. I'm not sure whether or not you can help us make wreaths, as that is the worst wreath I ever saw.
9. Where did you get that wretched pair of pants hanging around your waist? Whose are those weird things? They make you look as if you weigh an extra fifty pounds.
10. Hopefully, widespread advertising will bring a large group of women here to the meeting on Wednesday.

page 44

1. extinct
2. axis
3. exaggerate
4. examine
5. orthodox
6. complex
7. extravagant
8. exception
9. excite
10. exhale
11. excuse
12. excavate
13. reflex
14. extract
15. maximum
16. excess
17. complexion
18. exasperated

page 45

1. convey
2. antonym
3. canyon

4. bicycle
5. synonym
6. envy
7. myth
8. defy
9. rhythm
10. anonymous
11. rhyme
12. symptoms
13. canopy
14. hypothesis
15. paralysis
16. mystify
17. apathy
18. chewy

page 46

Across
3. hazard
4. seize
6. prize
8. apologize
12. ionize
14. quizzical
16. azure
18. haze
19. cozy
20. maize
21. rendezvous
23. laziness
24. buzzard

Down
1. craze
2. jeopardize
5. adz
7. realize
9. ozone
10. visualize
11. raze
13. blizzard
15. vocalize
17. razor
18. hypnotize
22. eczema

page 47

1. laugh
2. laughable
3. laughter
4. amusement
5. comedy
6. comedian
7. comic
8. giggle
9. chuckle
10. mirth
11. hilarious
12. joke or jest
13. humorous
14. humor
15. merriment
16. witty
17. amusing

18. wisecrack
19. mischief
20. buffoon
21. ridicule
22. prankster
23. ludicrous
24. amuse

page 48

1. Incredible!
2. Awesome!
3. Preposterous!
4. Unbelievable
5. Shocking news
6. Exceptional!
7. No trespassing
8. Be quiet
9. Unthinkable
10. National emergency!
11. Pay attention!
12. Irresistible!
13. Wow! Twelfth touchdown!
14. Hooray for me
15. Extravagant
16. Look out for the ambulance
17. Absolutely not!
18. Stop! Thief!
19. You're a nuisance
20. School is canceled!

page 49

February 6

Dear Abby,
I'm sorry you missed the show. Finally I have time to tell you about it.
It was an awkward trick for a gorilla, I admit, to climb onto a trapeze balancing an architect and an artichoke on opposite arms. Fortunately, we hired a talented gorilla. This may seem weird—not your obvious circus performance. But you have to admit, it was a unique idea. And certain people flocked to purchase expensive tickets.
The gorilla was a tame and calm one, with no obvious tendencies toward violence. He had practiced this trick many times, even performing it at a banquet before a group of famous politicians.
As the curtain went up and the show began, I was grateful that everything was going smoothly. And then—there was the mosquito that somehow got onto the gorilla's tongue. Our friendly pet turned fierce. In less than a minute, he swung down to the net, turned a huge somersault, and devoured the architect—whole, as an unbelieving crowd of spectators, including me, watched in horror.
Sorry you missed it.

Your friend,
Serena

page 50

1. CITIZENS BOYCOTT BROCCOLI
2. BUSINESSES BARELY AVOID TRAFFIC HAZARDS
3. EXERCISE WOULD HAVE BENEFITED DINOSAURS
4. CONGRESS CANCELS CALENDAR
5. COUNTERFEITER GETS FORTY YEARS
6. DIAMOND FOUND BURIED IN DOG BISCUITS
7. AMBULANCE RUSHES TO SCHOOL CAFETERIA
8. SENATOR ABSENT EVERY WEDNESDAY
9. BALLOON CROSSES PACIFIC
10. RESTAURANT LICENSE SUSPENDED
11. ARITHMETIC CAUSES INDIGESTION
12. ARTICHOKE CHOKES GORILLA